JOHN W. SCHAUM
NOTE SPELLER
Book Two

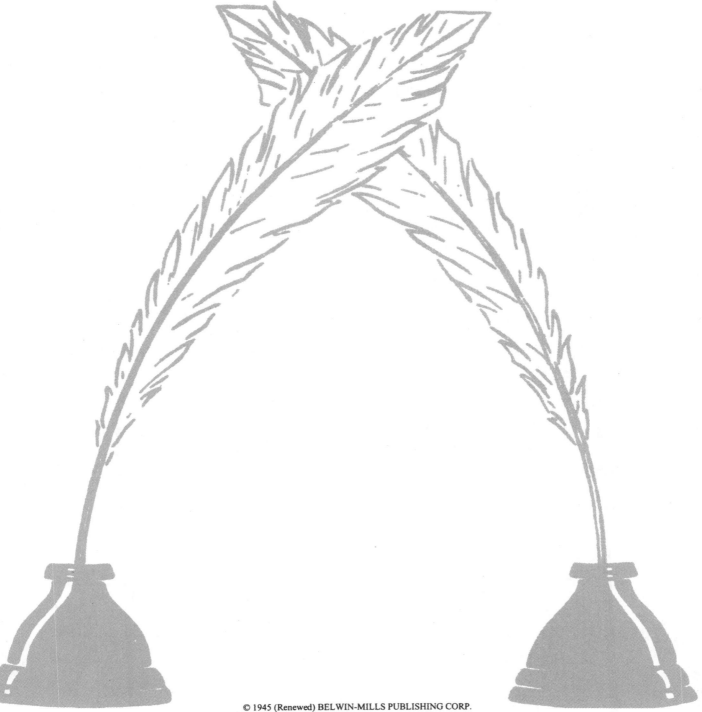

CONTENTS

Lesson 1. Tonality Spelling
(Key of G Major, one sharp: F♯)

Note to Teachers: A very common error in note reading is a failure to watch the sharps or flats in the key signature.
The first six lessons of the speller are devoted to tonality spelling to help the student remember the key signature.

DIRECTIONS: In the following measures, write the correct letter names. Remember you are in the key of G Major, so be sure to sharp every F. Study the sample.

(Sample)

F♯ E D ....

(Write letter names. Watch the key signature.)

Bass Clef

Lesson 2. Tonality Spelling
(Key of F Major, one flat: B♭)

DIRECTIONS: In the measures below, write the correct letter names. Remember you are in the key of F Major, so be sure to flat every B. Study the sample.

(Write letter names. Watch the new key signature.)

Lesson 3. Tonality Spelling
(Key of D Major, two sharps: F♯ and C♯)

DIRECTIONS: Write letter names as before, keeping in mind that the key signature is D Major. Study the sample. Notice the *brace* which connects the treble and bass staffs.

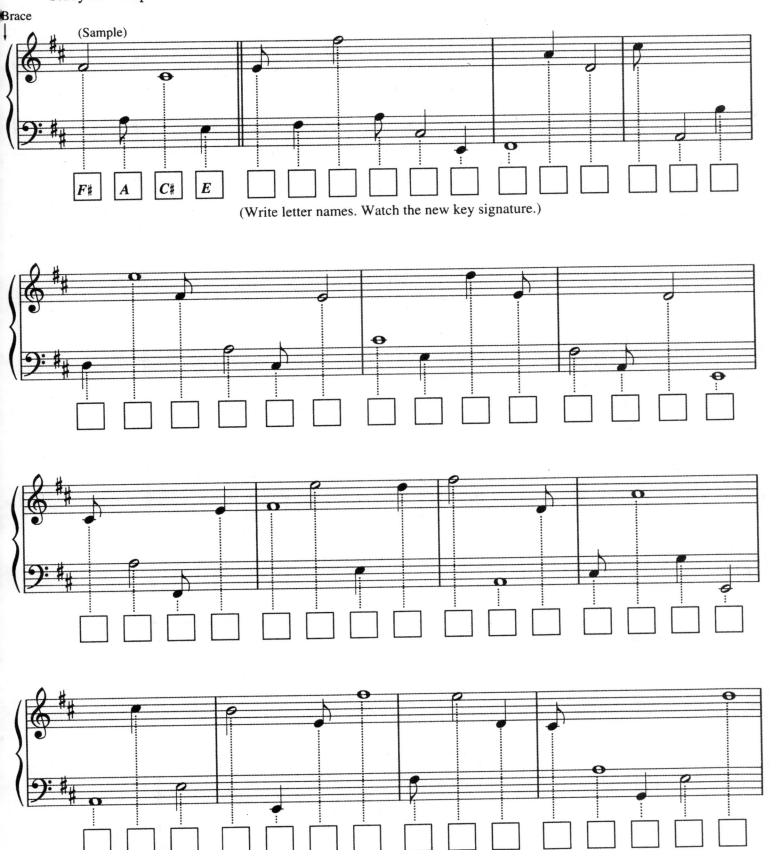

(Write letter names. Watch the new key signature.)

Lesson 4. Tonality Spelling
(Key of B♭ Major, two flats: B♭ and E♭)

DIRECTIONS: Write letter names, taking care to flat all the Bs and Es indicated in the B♭ Major key signature. Study the sample.

(Write letter names. Watch the new key signature.)

Lesson 5. Tonality Spelling
(Key of A Major, three sharps: F♯, C♯, and G♯)

DIRECTIONS: Write letter names, according to the key of A Major.
Watch the sharps indicated in the key signature.

(Write letter names. Watch the new key signature.)

Lesson 6. Tonality Spelling
(Key of E♭ Major, three flats: B♭, E♭, and A♭)

DIRECTIONS: Write the letter names, observing the three flats in the key signature of E♭ Major.

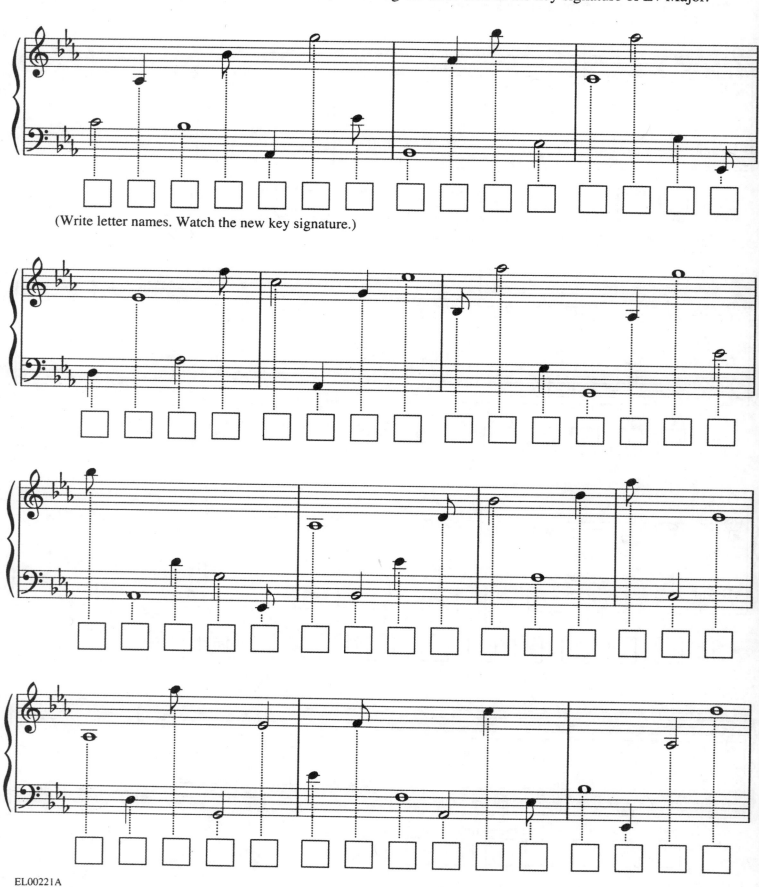

(Write letter names. Watch the new key signature.)

EL00221A

Lesson 7. Accidentals

(Key of C)

Note to Teachers: This lesson is designed to impress upon the pupil that a sharp, flat, or natural sign holds throughout a measure, and that a new measure invalidates it.

EXPLANATION: Sharps, flats and naturals not in the key signature are called ACCIDENTALS. An accidental affects every note which follows it *only on the same line or space,* within the same measure. A new measure automatically cancels the preceeding accidentals. As a precaution, reminder accidentals (sometimes in parenthesis) may be added in the next measure by a composer or music editor. However, reminder accidentals are not necessary.

DIRECTIONS: In each of the measures below, you will find accidentals. Write the correct letter names on the dotted lines. Study the sample.

(Write letter names. Watch for accidentals that carry over.)

Bass Clef

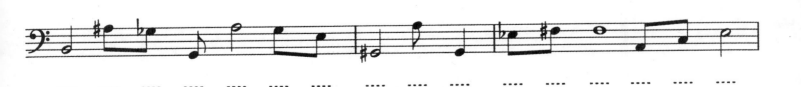

EL00221A

Lesson 8. Accidentals
(Other Keys)

EXPLANATION: Remember that an F sharp in the key signature affects *every* F, whether or not it is on the same line or space. In all other key signatures, the sharps or flats have the same effect. However, this is not so with accidentals; they affect only notes which follow *on the same line or space* within the same measure.

DIRECTIONS: Write the correct letter names on the dotted lines. Notice the various key signatures. Study the sample.

This F is also natural because of the preceding F natural.

(Sample)

B   A   F♮   F♮

(Write letter names. Natural signs must be included wherever necessary.)

Lesson 9. Ties and Slurs

A TIE is a curved line joining two notes next to each other *on the same line or space*. The second note is not played, but is held for its time value.

A SLUR is a curved line joining any number of successive notes on various lines and spaces. The notes within a slur form a phrase and should be connected by playing smoothly.

DIRECTIONS: Below is a series of ties and slurs. In the boxes, write T for *tie* or S for *slur*.

Lesson 10. Inner Leger Lines

(Below Treble and Above Bass)

EXPLANATION: In finding leger notes, always think in terms of LINES. Notice that from line to line there is always a skip of one white key on the piano (or a skip of one letter name). To find leger line notes *under* the treble staff, start at the bottom line (E) and go DOWN. To find leger line notes *above* the bass staff, start at the top line (A) and go UP.

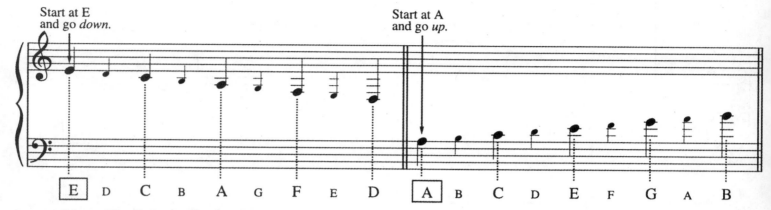

(Note: The line notes and letters are larger.)

DIRECTIONS: Using the chart above, find each note at the keyboard first; then write the letter names in the squares.

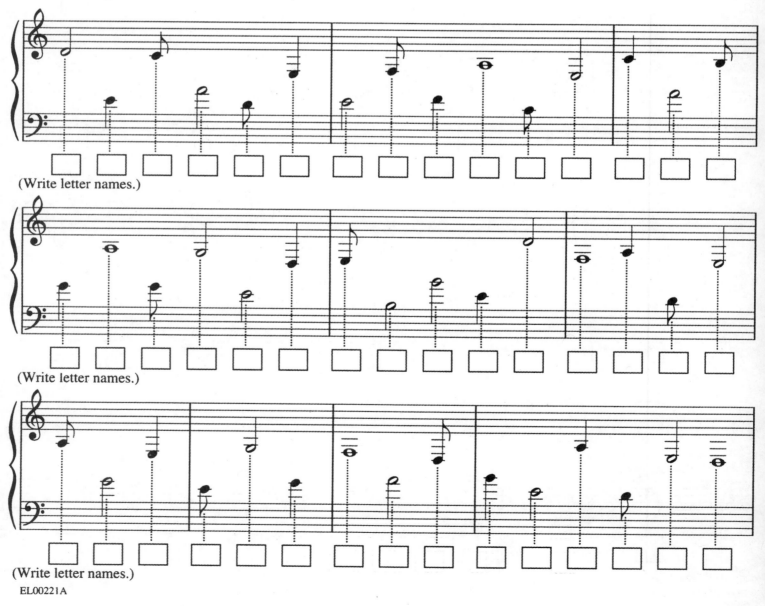

(Write letter names.)

(Write letter names.)

(Write letter names.)

EL00221A

Lesson 11. Inner Leger Lines
(continued)

Write letter names in the squares below. (See chart in Lesson 10.)

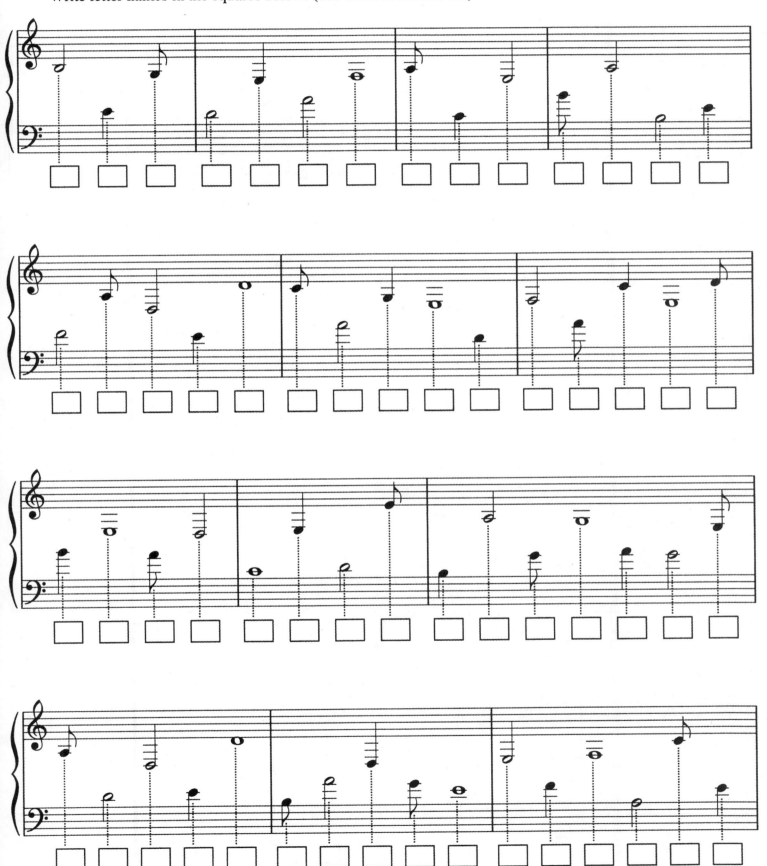

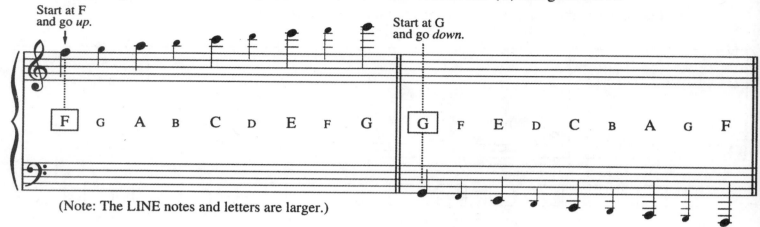

Lesson 12. Outer Leger Lines
(Above Treble and Below Bass)

EXPLANATION: To find leger line notes *above* the treble staff, start at the top line (F) and go UP. To find leger line notes *below* the bass staff, start at the bottom line (G) and go DOWN.

(Note: The LINE notes and letters are larger.)

DIRECTIONS: Using the chart above, find each note at the keyboard first; then write the letter names in the squares. These directions also apply to Lesson 13.

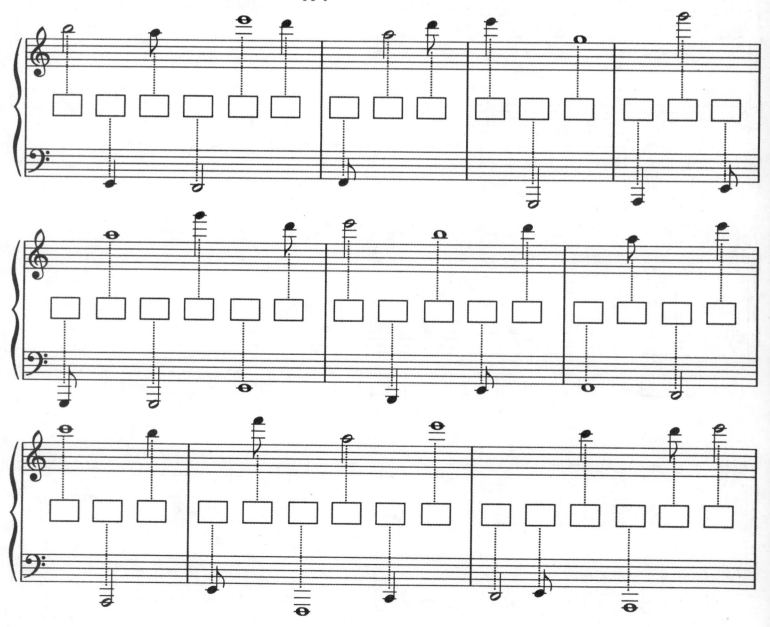

Lesson 13. Outer Leger Lines

(continued)

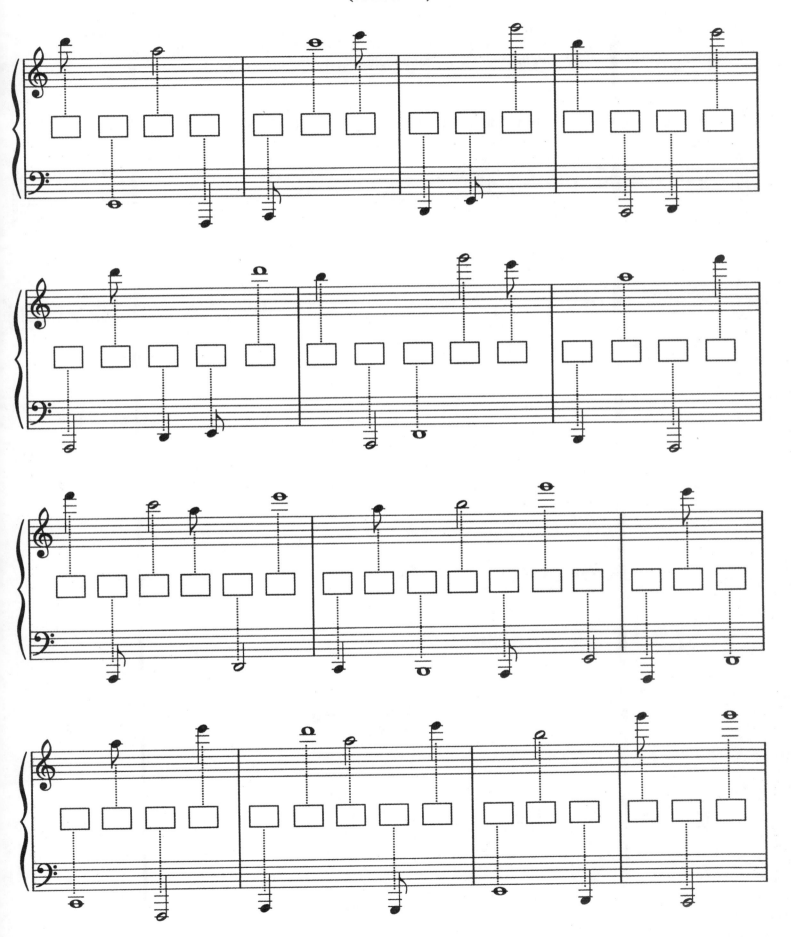

Lesson 14. Identifying Intervals

EXPLANATION: An interval is the distance from one note to another. For example, the interval from G to B is a 3rd because it includes 3 letter names, G-A-B. To find an interval, add up the total number of letter names, *starting with the bottom note* and including the top note. Study the samples.

DIRECTIONS: Write the interval number beneath each of the following intervals.

Lesson 15. Writing Intervals

DIRECTIONS: Above each of the following notes, draw a note to make the interval that is indicated by the number. In the first example, 3 above E is G, so the note G is placed on the second staff line as shown. Draw whole notes to form each interval. Study the samples.

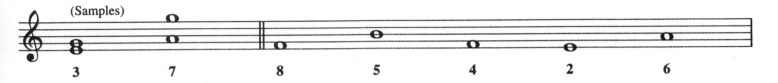

(Samples)

3   7   8   5   4   2   6

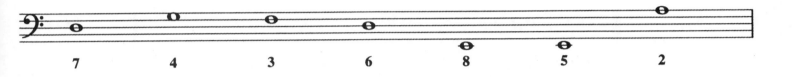

7   4   3   6   8   5   2

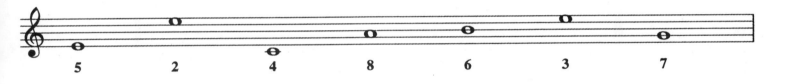

5   2   4   8   6   3   7

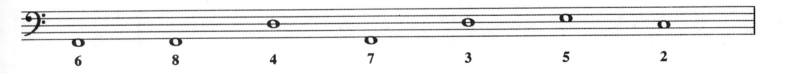

6   8   4   7   3   5   2

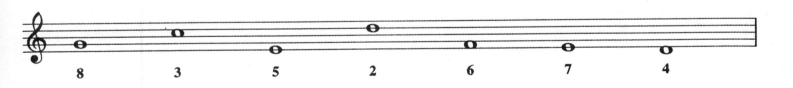

8   3   5   2   6   7   4

5   4   7   3   6   8   2

Lesson 16. The Use of Dots

EXPLANATION: Dots are used in music for two purposes: first, to indicate *staccato;* second, to *lengthen* a note. When placed *above or below* a note, a dot indicates STACCATO, meaning to strike the note with a quick release. When placed *after* a note, a dot LENGTHENS the value of the note.

DIRECTIONS: Below is a series of dotted notes. Write S for *staccato;* write L if the dot *lengthens* the note. Study the samples.

Lesson 17. The Dot After a Note

DIRECTIONS: A dot placed after a note adds HALF the value of the note to it. In each of the squares below, write a note which is *equal* in value to the DOT. Study the samples.

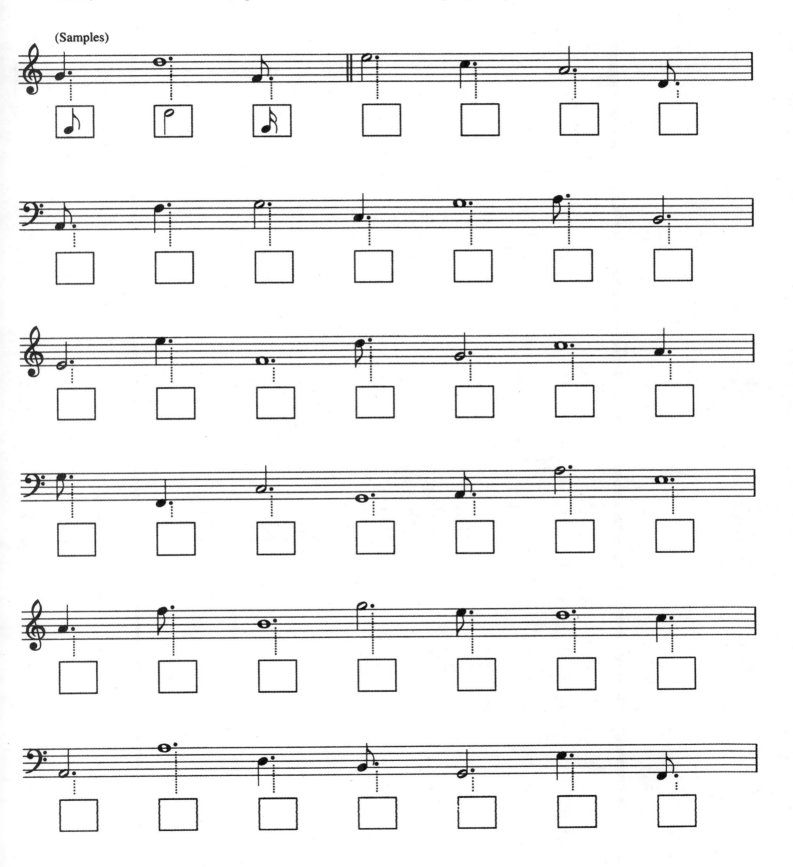

Lesson 18. The Dot After a Rest

DIRECTIONS: Rests occasionally have dots after them. A dot placed after a rest adds HALF the value of the rest to it. In each of the squares below, draw a rest which is *equal* in value to the DOT. Study the samples.

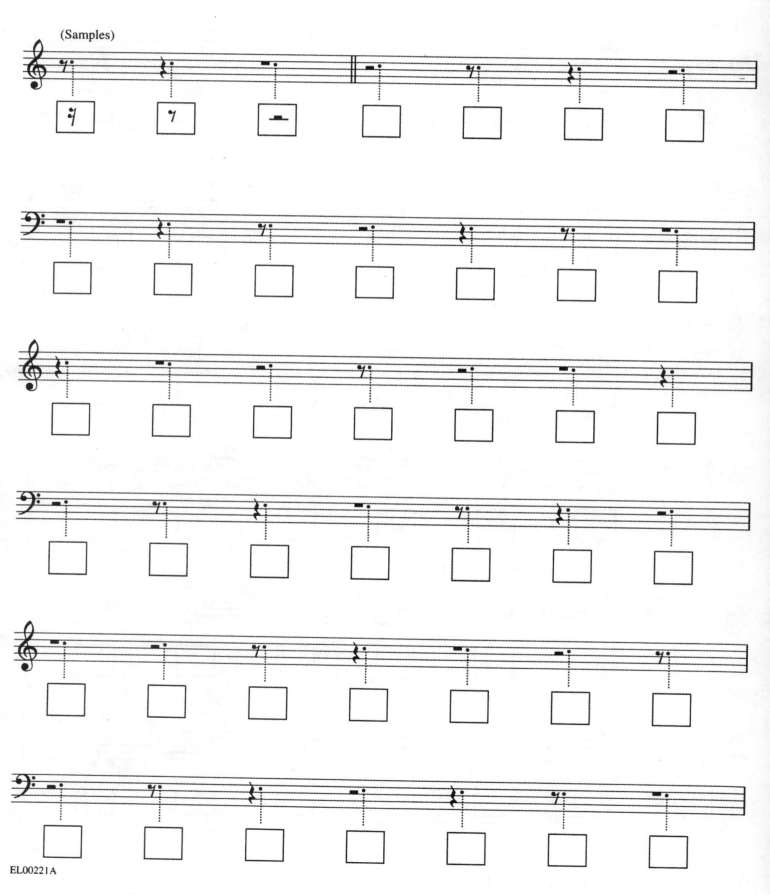

Lesson 19. The Double Dot

EXPLANATION: When a note has two dots after it, the first dot adds one half of its value; the second dot adds one quarter of its value. Study these examples:

DIRECTIONS: Notice the time signature in each of the following staffs, and draw measure bar lines where needed. (Do not write letter names.) Study the samples.

(Samples)

EL00221A

Lesson 20. Identifying Triplets

EXPLANATION: A triplet is a way of dividing a note into three equal parts. A triplet is indicated with a slur or bracket and an italic number *3*. For example, when three half notes are joined with a bracket and italic number *3*, together they equal a *whole* note. Study the chart below for other triplet combinations.

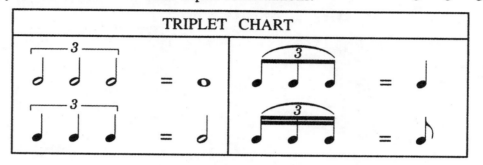

DIRECTIONS: In the squares below, write one note that *equals* each of the following triplets. Study the samples.

Lesson 21. Further Triplet Study

Triplets sometimes occur in combination with rests. In each square below write a REST equal in time value to the triplet directly above it. Study the samples.

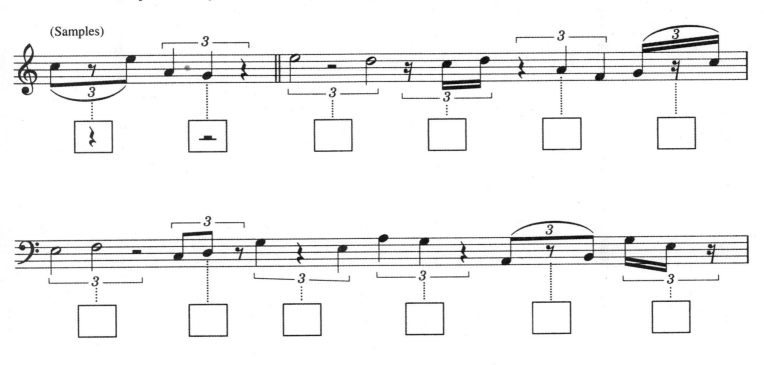

On the staffs below, write a triplet equal to each of the given notes. Study the sample.

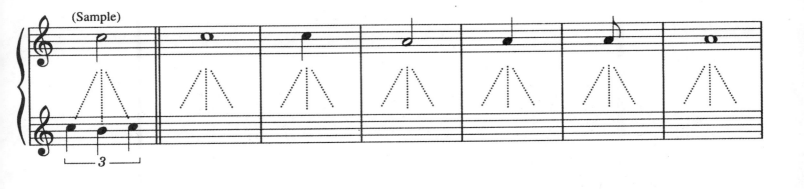

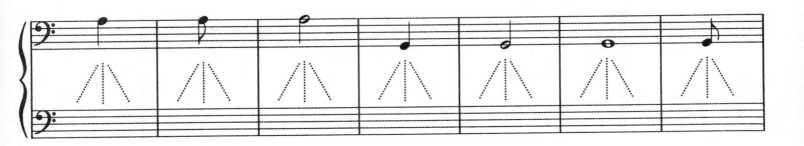

EL00221A

Lesson 22. Double Sharps and Double Flats

This sign (✗) is a *double sharp* and raises a note one whole step.
This sign (♭♭) is a *double flat* and lowers a note one whole step.

DIRECTIONS: Write another letter name for each of the following notes. For example, the first note in the staff below is F double sharp. Another name for F double sharp is G natural; therefore, write G♮ (or just plain G) on the dotted line. Study the samples.

Lesson 23 — Review of Time Signatures

> Reminder: The two large numbers at the beginning of a staff are the *time signature*. For example:
>
> **3** The *upper* number tells us HOW MANY counts in a measure - in this case, three.
> **4** The *lower* number tells us WHAT KIND of note gets one count - in this case, a quarter note.
>
> The symbol **C** is sometimes used to represent 4/4 (common time).
>
> The sign **¢** represents 2/2 time (cut time).

DIRECTIONS: Below are eighteen questions about time signatures. Write the correct answer after each question. Use notation and numbers in the answers.

Answer Column

1. Draw the kind of note that gets one count in 4/4 time. . . . . 1. _____

2. How many counts to a measure in 3/4 time? . . . . 2. _____

3. Draw the note that gets one count in 3/2 time. . . . . 3. _____

4. How many counts to a measure in **¢** time? . . . . 4. _____

5. Draw the note that gets one count in **C** time. . . . . 5. _____

6. How many counts to a measure in 9/8 time? . . . . 6. _____

7. Draw the note that gets one count in 6/8 time. . . . . 7. _____

8. How many counts to a measure in 2/4 time? . . . . 8. _____

9. Draw the note that gets one count in 3/8 time. . . . . 9. _____

10. How many counts to a measure in 3/2 time? . . . . 10. _____

11. Draw the note that gets one count in 3/4 time. . . . . 11. _____

12. How many counts to a measure in 6/8 time? . . . . 12. _____

13. Draw the note that gets one count in **¢** time. . . . . 13. _____

14. How many counts to a measure in 4/4 time? . . . . 14. _____

15. Draw the note that gets one count in 9/8 time. . . . . 15. _____

16. How many counts to a measure in **C** time? . . . . 16. _____

17. Draw the note that gets one count in 2/4 time. . . . . 17. _____

18. How many counts to a measure in 3/8 time? . . . . 18. _____

Lesson 24. Correcting Counting Errors

DIRECTIONS: The melody of "Juanita" is printed below. One measure is crossed out because the number of counts in incorrect. Nine other measures have mistakes. Play through the tune and cross out the *nine* wrong measures.

DIRECTIONS: Play through the melody of "Lightly Row" below and cross out the *six* wrong measures.

Lesson 25. Identifying Time Signatures

DIRECTIONS: Below are ten complete measures. To the right of each are five time signatures. Circle the proper time signature for each example. **Study the sample.**

Sample: The time signature is $\frac{4}{4}$ $\left(\frac{3}{4}\right)$ $\frac{6}{8}$ $\frac{3}{8}$ $\frac{2}{4}$

1. The time signature is $\frac{9}{8}$ $\frac{4}{4}$ $\frac{3}{8}$ $\frac{2}{4}$ $\frac{3}{4}$

2. The time signature is $\frac{6}{8}$ ¢ $\frac{3}{4}$ $\frac{2}{4}$ $\frac{3}{8}$

3. The time signature is $\frac{2}{4}$ $\frac{6}{8}$ $\frac{3}{4}$ $\frac{4}{4}$ $\frac{3}{8}$

4. The time signature is $\frac{4}{4}$ $\frac{6}{8}$ $\frac{2}{4}$ $\frac{3}{4}$ $\frac{3}{8}$

5. The time signature is $\frac{3}{2}$ $\frac{9}{8}$ $\frac{6}{8}$ $\frac{3}{4}$ C

6. The time signature is $\frac{3}{4}$ $\frac{4}{4}$ $\frac{6}{8}$ $\frac{3}{2}$ $\frac{2}{4}$

7. The time signature is $\frac{3}{8}$ $\frac{4}{4}$ $\frac{6}{8}$ $\frac{3}{2}$ ¢

8. The time signature is $\frac{2}{4}$ $\frac{3}{8}$ $\frac{4}{4}$ $\frac{3}{4}$ $\frac{9}{8}$

9. The time signature is C $\frac{3}{8}$ $\frac{3}{4}$ $\frac{6}{8}$ $\frac{3}{2}$

10. The time signature is $\frac{3}{4}$ $\frac{9}{8}$ $\frac{4}{4}$ $\frac{2}{4}$ $\frac{6}{8}$

Lesson 26. Measure Completion (Notes)

DIRECTIONS: A note has been omitted from each of the measures below. Circle the correct note which completes the measure. Study the sample.

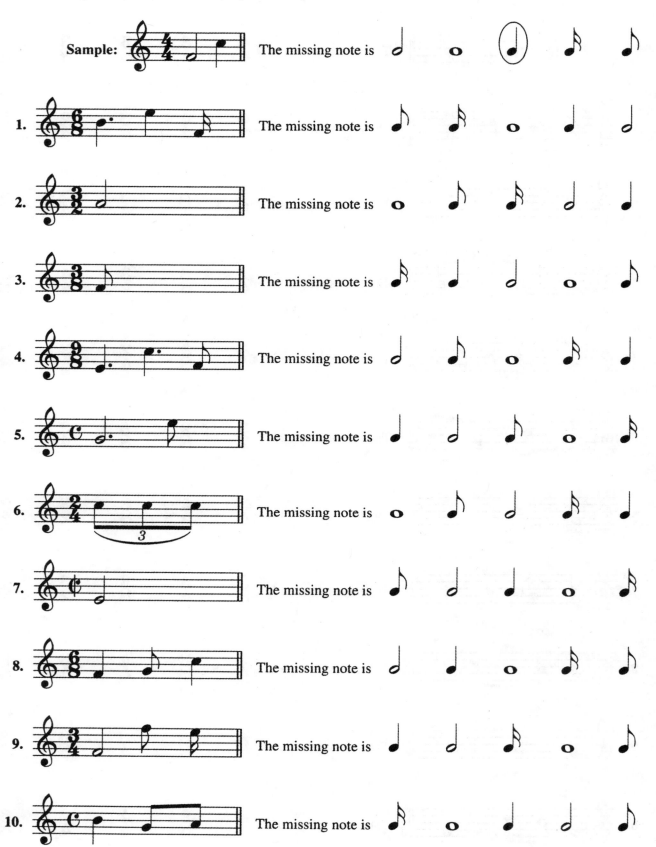

Lesson 27. Measure Completion (Rests)

DIRECTIONS: A *rest* has been omitted from each of the measures below. Circle the correct rest which completes the measure. Study the sample.

Lesson 28. Inserting Time Signatures

EXPLANATION: In each of the measures below, add up the total number of counts and determine the proper time signature. In the case of 6/8 time and 3/4 time, the difference is in the way beams are used to connect and group the notes. Study the following illustrations:

This is a measure in
$\frac{6}{8}$ time.

This is a measure in
$\frac{3}{4}$ time.

DIRECTIONS: Write the correct time signature in each of the following measures.

The time signatures used are: $\frac{4}{4}$, $\frac{6}{8}$, $\frac{3}{4}$, $\frac{2}{4}$.

EL00221A

Lesson 29. Placing Measure Bar Lines

DIRECTIONS: Below are several lines of notes. Add measure bar lines where needed to make the correct number of counts in each measure. Watch the time signatures. Study the samples.

After
Book Two
of the
SCHAUM
NOTE SPELLER

use John W. Schaum's
HARMONY LESSONS
IN TWO VOLUMES

Schaum Harmony Lessons can be used by instrumental, vocal and piano teachers who want their students to know some of the essentials of harmony, but who haven't the time to teach it as a separate subject. Thus a piano teacher, for example, can teach harmony in conjunction with the regular piano lesson.

The lessons are in workbook form, eliminating the need for an extra pad of music paper. Space is provided for all written assignments in the book itself.

There is a test at the end of each book to check on the retention of the subject matter.

At the end of Book II, we have employed harmony as an accompaniment rather than as traditional four-part harmony.

Transposition has been treated both melodically and harmonically.